ACTIVATING VOCABULARY

Contents

Photocopy for BRAIN-friendly language fun!

You will find Flexible Friends Vocabulary Cards ISBN 1 898295 11 5 a useful class and self-access resource for further practice.

© English Experience, 25 Julian Road, Folkestone, Kent, CT19 5HW

Brain-*friendly* activities for Activating Vocabulary
(Relevant units in brackets)

Introducing the topic (All) Use photographs/magazine pictures or other realia to stimulate interest and curiosity. Tell a little story/anecdote which 'drops in' some new vocabulary the student will meet in the unit.

Matching - words to pictures (All) Encourage students to write on the worksheet. Play Question and Answer games 'Can you tell me number seven please?' in pairs and/or around the class.

Category pictures (5B, 6B, 7B, 8C, 13E, 20C) Encourage students to use coloured felt tips to underline words which 'go together' and write them in the picture categories. In teams, brainstorm new words for each category.

Mind Maps (1D, 2D, 3D, 6E 10D, 15E) Students jot down key words on the Mind Map given with each unit. They use the Mind Map as the basis for a short talk to a neighbour. Ask individuals to give a short talk to the whole class.

Mixed definitions (6C, 17C) These are good for expanding vocabulary. Encourage small groups to brainstorm new examples to test their colleagues.

'Odd one out' (1C, 4B, 9C, 11C) Students need to explain why one word is chosen as the 'odd one out' - (usually there are alternatives, and different students will find different reasons for their choice). This is an easy exercise to extend by brainstorming new sets.

Story telling (All) Having done the 'matching' activities, each student chooses any 3 words (new or interesting ones) and writes a very simple story/paragraph which incorporates them.

Careful listening (All) Following on from **Storytelling**, one student reads the paragraph to a partner. The partner must identify the three 'special words' incorporated in the story.

Interviews/ role plays can be generated by most units, (especially 1D, 2D, 3D, 6E, 10D, 11E, 12C, 13F, 15E, 16D). Read through the functional language and set up a simple shopping / holiday / visit to the Doctor situation.

Step 9

Music (All) Near the end of the lesson, put on some relaxing music. The students settle quietly, while the teacher reads through the target words and phrases again – slowly enough to allow them to echo in the memory.

Step 10

Posters (All - and especially the category pictures units) Students put words onto cards and arrange them in categories to make a colourful reminder. Make a big version of the Mind Maps. This is good activity for kinaesthetic and visual learners.

Step 11

Movement/Mime/Acting (4A, 5C, 9A+D, 10A, 12C, 16A,17A, 20A) Wherever possible encourage students to exchange information and to 'act out' situations in English. For example, guessing the actions (5C) or putting on a Fashion Show (12C).

Step 12

Presentations and discussions (2C, 6D, 9D, 10C, 11E, 12C, 17F) Encourage individuals, or teams, to present something of interest - for example their town or their hobby, and ensure that the others ask questions about it.

Step 13

Puzzles (12B, 13B, 15B) Give these a competitive edge by setting a tight time limit. It's easy to make similar examples for other units.

Step 14

Writing (All - especially 17F, 10C, 14C, 16A, 19B+C) Some units contain specific writing activities and they all lend themselves to a 'write a postcard about...' exercise.

Step 15

Fun with Pronunciation (All) In each unit select, say, six words. Focus on the pronunciation and syllable stress. Say them singly, slowly, fast, in a list, beating out a stress pattern. Put several into a sentence and practice it as a statement / a question / pleasantly / angrily.

Step 16

The **more contacts** – and the greater the **variety of contacts** and associations – that the brain makes with new information, the better the likelihood of transfer from short to **long term memory**. Use as many of these approaches as possible with each exercise. Repetition, recycling, is still one of the most effective ways to remember vocabulary, so use the poster idea as an ongoing peripheral and 'revisit' the topics from time to time. Personalise each topic, and look out for any opportunity to bring in colour, movement, sound, humour and the bizarre.

Happy activating!

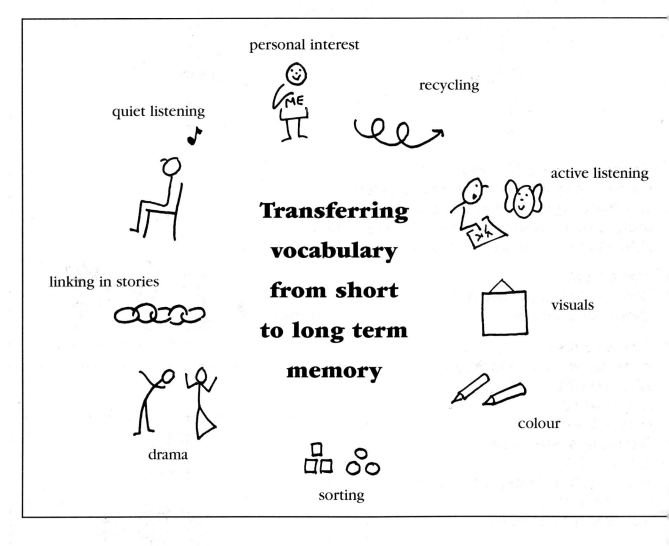

personal interest

recycling

quiet listening

active listening

Transferring vocabulary from short to long term memory

visuals

linking in stories

colour

drama

sorting

The introduction to *Activating Vocabulary* touches briefly on BRAIN-*friendly* methodology. For a much fuller account of the theory and practice please read the *English Experience* title called *Teaching for Success* by Mark Fletcher ISBN 1 898295 62 X

A **Are you married?**
No I'm not.

Have you got any brothers and sisters?
I've got two older sisters and a younger brother.
How old is your brother?
He's fifteen.

B **WORD CHECK**

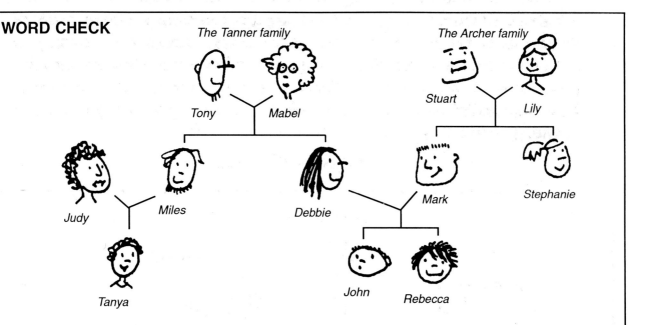

The Tanner family

Tony *Mabel*

Judy *Miles* *Debbie* *Mark*

Tanya *John* *Rebecca*

The Archer family

Stuart *Lily*

Stephanie

Relatives – the family tree
husband, wife, mother, father, son, daughter
grandfather, grandmother, grandson, granddaughter
uncle, aunt, nephew, niece, cousin, daughter-in-law
sister-in-law, brother-in-law, mother-in-law, father-in-law

Who's who?
How quickly can you find out?
(these words will help)

*Other members of
the family – pets!*

Tony is Mark's ...
What relation is John to Stuart? ...
Who is Mark's niece? ...
Judy is Miles' ...
Miles is Mark's ...
Stephanie is Rebecca's ...
John and Tanya are ...
What relation is Rebecca to Judy? ...
Debbie is Lily's ...
Has John got an uncle? ...

D

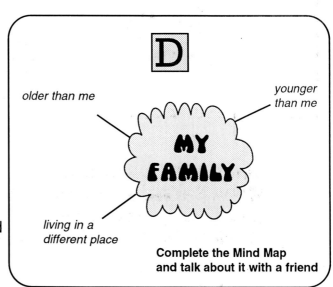

older than me

younger
than me

**MY
FAMILY**

living in a
different place

**Complete the Mind Map
and talk about it with a friend**

C **ODD ONE OUT**
<u>aunt</u> – father-in-law – grandfather – husband

• nephew – niece – son – cousin
• wife – daughter – uncle – grandmother
• goldfish – sister – brother – father

Activating Vocabulary – My Family

2 MY TOWN

A WORD CHECK

① ② ③ ④ ⑤ ⑥

village... medium sized town... old city... industrial city... port... modern city...

B Where do you live?

I live in ....   It's an industrial town.

Can I visit you?   *You're very welcome.*

It's
- a small town.
- a village.
- an old city.
- a modern city.
- a port.

- in...
- near...
- on the coast of...
- on the River...

How many people live there?   The population is about .... thousand.

What's the countryside like?   The countryside is
- very pretty.
- rather dull.

mountainous

flat   *hilly*

built-up

What sort of town is it?

The town has
- a university.
- good shops.
- a good night life.
- an interesting old port.
- lots of places to visit.

It's very
- quiet.
- busy.

It's full of
- factories.
- traffic
- tourists.
- students.
- retired people.

What do people do?   Most people
- work in an office/a factory.
- commute to the big cities.

Is there much to do in the evenings?

There
- is a lot to do.
- isn't much to do.

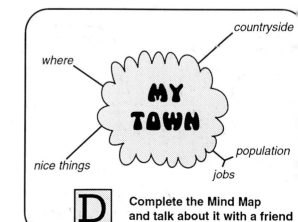

where   *countryside*

MY TOWN

nice things   *population*   *jobs*

C What is the best town you know?
Why do you like it?

D Complete the Mind Map and talk about it with a friend

ACTIVATING VOCABULARY – MY TOWN

© **English Experience, 25 Julian Road, Folkestone, Kent, CT19 5HW**

A I live in (town). **My home is** { two kilometres from / very near / not far from } { the town centre. / the harbour. / the shopping centre. }

B I live in a { terraced house... / detached house... / flat/apartment... } { palace... / hut... / castle... }

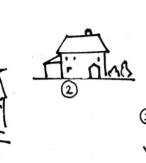

What's it like? { It has a big garden. / There isn't a garden. }

It's { old/modern. / quiet/noisy / comfortable/uncomfortable. / tidy/untidy. }

WORD CHECK

gate ... drive ... chimney ...

roof ... garage ... front door ... wall ...

path ... window ... satellite dish ...

C **Which is which?** downstairs ... dining room ... cellar ... upstairs ... attic ... bathroom ... living room ... toilet ... kitchen ... bedroom ... stairs ... lift/elevator ... third floor ...

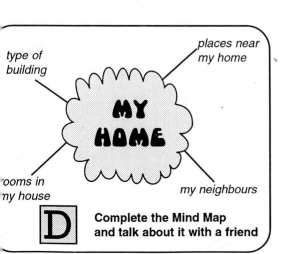

type of building

places near my home

MY HOME

rooms in my house

my neighbours

D Complete the Mind Map and talk about it with a friend

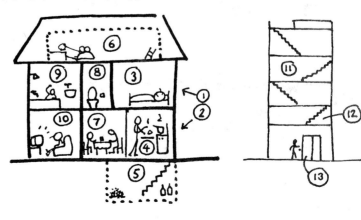

ACTIVATING VOCABULARY – MY HOME

4

Activating Vocabulary – In The House

A   WORD CHECK

I'll show you round my house. In the living room there is . . .

B

Find ten things you have in YOUR home. Tell a friend.

bedside table ... basin ... vegetable garden ... bookshelf ... mirror ... dishwasher ... teatowel hedge ... toilet ... shed ... sink ... lamp ... wardrobe ... armchair ... flower bed ... fireplace ... refrigerator ... fence ... lawn ... pillow ... cupboard ... sofa ... sheet ... cooker ... rug ... bath chest of drawers ... carpet ... greenhouse ... oven ... blanket ... coffee table ... tap ... shower ... ornaments ... microwave ... curtains ... dressing gown ... hangers ...

B   ODD ONE OUT
- cooker – sink – basin – bath
- cupboard – chair – drawer – wardrobe
- carpet – rug – mat – mirror
- fence – shed – wall – hedge
- shower – tap – sheet – bath

A WORD CHECK

car... bike... lorry... ambulance... motorbike...van... bus... fire engine... coach... people carrier...

nd these buildings....?

block of flats... bus station... building site... factory... row of houses...
row of shops... modern estate... office block... warehouse... church ...

B

Put the
words into
the right
categories
(5 in each)

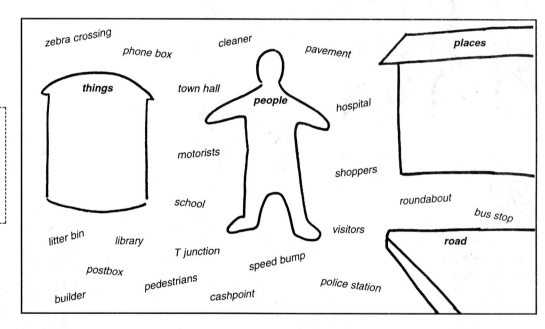

zebra crossing
phone box
cleaner
pavement
places

things
town hall
people
hospital

motorists
shoppers

school
roundabout
bus stop

litter bin
library
visitors
road

T junction
speed bump

postbox
pedestrians
police station

builder
cashpoint

C WORD CHECK – What are they doing?

tting on a bench ...
etting on a bus ...
ushing the baby buggy ...
ding a bike ...
osting a letter ...
riving a car ...
aking a phone call ...
uying some fruit ...
king the dog for a walk ...
aiting (queuing) for a bus ...
rossing the road ...
oking in the window ...
lking/chatting ...
etting off a bus ...

ACTIVATING VOCABULARY – IN THE STREET

A WORD CHECK

farm ... hill ... lake ... mountain ... field ... waterfall ... forest ... bridge ... river ... wood ... stream

On the farm

tractor... barn... farmhouse... stable... pigsty... workers... pond... muck heap...

B

Put the words into the right categories (5 in each)

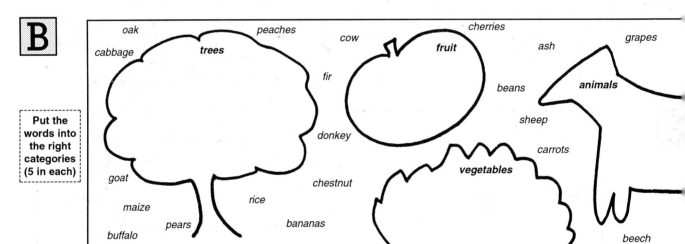

oak   peaches   cow   cherries   ash   grapes
cabbage   *trees*   *fruit*   *animals*
fir   beans
donkey   sheep
goat   carrots
chestnut   *vegetables*
maize   rice
pears   bananas
buffalo   beech

C These are mixed up! Make the right connections –

	trees	flock
	sheep	range
	birds	crowd
A lot of	mountains	is a flock
	cows	forest
	tourists	herd

D Use the Mind Map to describe the countryside near your home. Is it . . .
hilly/mountainous/flat/wooded/grassy/
desert/rocky/marshy?
Are there a lot of
fields/lanes/streams/plantations/lakes?
What grows in the area?
What do you like/dislike about living in the country?

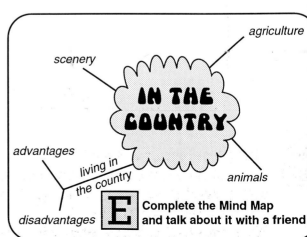

scenery   agriculture

IN THE COUNTRY

advantages   living in the country   animals

disadvantages

E Complete the Mind Map and talk about it with a friend

© **English Experience, 25 Julian Road, Folkestone, Kent, CT19 5HW**

A WORD CHECK

harbour... horizon... waves... rocks... pushchair...
wind surfer... beach... fishing boat... fish...
sunbathers... cliff... castle... lighthouse... life belt ...
stall... ferry... sailing boat... deck chair... seagulls...
cloud... hotels... mermaid... palm trees ...
water skier... island... beach hut... speedboat ...

B

Put the words into the right categories (6 in each)

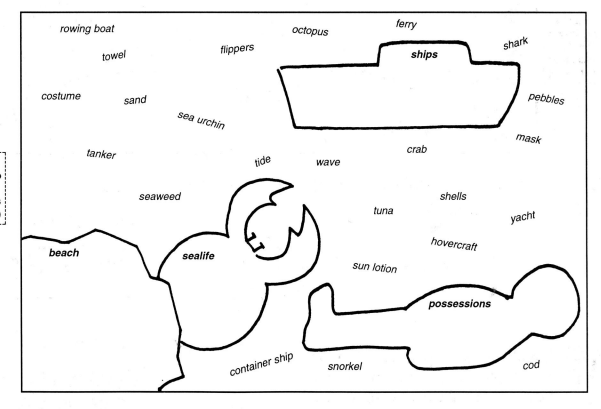

rowing boat
towel
octopus
ferry
ships
shark
flippers
costume
sand
sea urchin
pebbles
mask
crab
tanker
tide
wave
seaweed
shells
tuna
yacht
hovercraft
beach
sealife
sun lotion
possessions
container ship
snorkel
cod

C

Things to do at the seaside:
You can relax/sunbathe/go swimming/diving/snorkelling/
collect shells/play on the beach/go fishing
What do you like to do?
Have you had any good/terrible holidays by the sea?

ACTIVATING VOCABULARY – AT THE SEASIDE

A

Ask the person next to you about their watch, bag, pen, coat, or something else.

That's a nice (hat)

How much { did it cost? / was it? }

Where did you { get it? / buy it? }

In the shop

Can I help you? { Just looking thanks / Yes, have you got a...? / Can I try this on please? / Can I have a look at that one? }

Where to shop...

Supermarket (large shop – basically for food but often sells other things as well) long rows of shelves, trolleys, wire baskets, special offers, wide range of goods, check-out counters.

Which is the cheapest/most expensive/best value?

leather £8

leather handmade large size £8

plastic £6

paper £3

Shopping Mall (one big building with lots of shops inside).

Corner Shop (little shop often owned and run by a family, personal service).

Market (Indoor/outdoor - usually lots of stalls). You can bargain for things.

Going shopping

shopping centre, window shopping, sale, bargain, very good value, reduced, shopping lis receipt, pay cash, pay by cheque, pay by credit card.

B

WORD CHECK

Where are these people
– and how are they shopping?

1 ....   2 ....   3 ....   4 ....   5 ....   6 ....

C

Where can you buy these things? 4 in each shop.

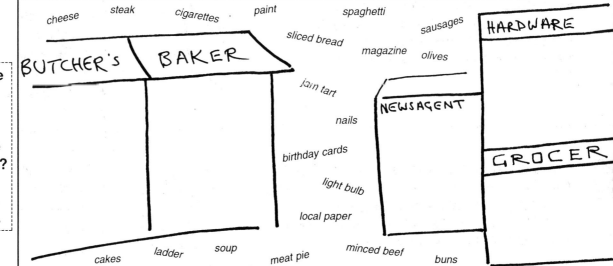

cheese   steak   cigarettes   paint   spaghetti

sliced bread   sausages   HARDWARE

magazine   olives

BUTCHER'S   BAKER

jam tart

nails   NEWSAGENT

birthday cards

GROCER

light bulb

local paper

cakes   ladder   soup   meat pie   minced beef   buns

A WORD CHECK

stick...

court...

winning post...

baton...

pads...

bowling alley...

club...

diving board...

ring...

bat...

net...

helmet...

pool...

pitch...

track...

wicket...

weights...

What sports not shown here are important in your country?

B

Can you describe (or demonstrate) the following events?
hurdles/relay/marathon/putting the shot/
throwing the discus/pole vault

C ODD ONE OUT

- ice hockey – field hockey – football – table tennis
- swimming – water polo – diving – basketball
- wrestling – judo – gymnastics – boxing
- discus – javelin – hammer – long jump
- spectator – referee – umpire – judge
- stadium – sponsor – track – pitch

Olympic Programme

1. Archery
2. Athletics
3. Basketball
4. Boxing
5. Canoeing
6. Cycling
7. Equestrian Riding
8. Football
9. Gymnastics
10. Judo
11. Pentathlon
12. Rowing
13. Shooting
14. Volleyball
15. Water Polo
16. Weight Lifting
17. Yachting

D

You are the Policy Committee of the Olympic Council.
The Olympic Games are too big and too expensive.
Your task is to reduce the programme.
Decide which five events should be omitted
from the programme, and why!

ACTIVATING VOCABULARY – SPORTS

A In pairs discuss your hobbies, using the language below:

What are your interests/hobbies?
What do you do in your spare time?

I like
I'm keen on
I'm interested in
I'm good at
I enjoy

photography, dressmaking
food and wine, cooking
sailing, fishing, gardening,
playing badminton/chess
/the piano, singing, painting
listening to music,
collecting....., skateboarding
going to the cinema/theatre

Do you like competitions?
Why do you like it so much?

I do it for fun/for enjoyment/for my own interest/
for relaxation/to take my mind off work

B WORD CHECK

What hobbies do you connect with these pictures?
Which is   a) the most expensive?   b) the most dangerous?

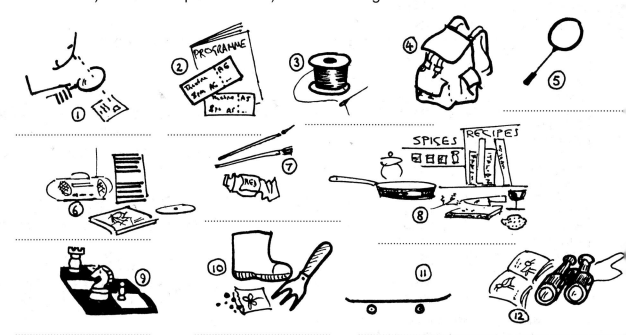

C **Think of words and phrases to help you describe your hobby to the class.**
Does it take a lot of time/money/practice/concentration?

Who is your favourite sportsman/
composer/painter/actress ...?

My favourite . . .

What do you need *for* { **football?**
{ **dressmaking?**

Kit: boots, shorts, etc.
Sewing equipment, material, etc.

How do you make (pottery)?

First you....., and then you.....

D

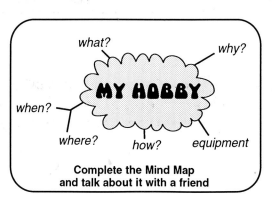

what?
why?
MY HOBBY
when?
where?   how?   equipment

Complete the Mind Map
and talk about it with a friend

E Which member of your class
has the most unusual hobby?

ACTIVATING VOCABULARY – HOBBIES

A What's the weather like? cloudy? snowy? windy? sunny? rainy? cold? foggy?

weather forecast

It's ....

What's the weather like in ... January? April? July? October?
(Of course, it may be 'changeable')

dull	cold	fine	stormy	humid
cloudy	snow and ice	bright and sunny	thunder and lightning	hot and wet (sticky)
grey	frost	warm	wind and rain	

B Which is the hottest/coldest country?
What time of year do you think it is?

```
WEATHER CHART
                °C                       °C
Algeria      s  21    Malta        s   18
Amsterdam    c   0    Montreal     s  -11
Athens       c  10    Moscow       sn  -9
Belgrade     2  -5    Munich       s   -4
Buenos Aires s  25    New York     s    1
Brussels     c   1    Nice         c   12
Cologne      f   0    Oslo         c   -7
Copenhagen   f   2    Paris        fg   3
Edinburgh    c   0    Reykjavik    c    2
Geneva       c   3    Rome         s   15
Helsinki     2  -6    Rome         s   15
Innsbruck    f   2    Stockholm    s   -4
Las Palmas   s  20    Tel Aviv     s   18
London       s   3    Toronto      s   -9
Madrid       f  14    Vienna       s   -6
Malaga       s  19    Zurich       c   -1

      Key:  c = cloudy   f = fair   r = rain
            s = sunny   sn = snow   fg = fog
```

C ODD ONE OUT

• freezing – humid – icy – cold
• tornado – breeze – rainbow – hurricane
• drought – shower – flood – rain
• fog – cloud – mist – avalanche

The weather is an important subject in England

Nice/lovely day
Warm/hot today   isn't it?
Chilly/horrible day

Yes it is, isn't it.

*Red sky at night, shepherd's delight.
Red sky in the morning, shepherd's warning!*

It never rains but it pours!

Every cloud has a silver lining.

Do you know any other weather proverbs?

 D Which countries have these weather conditions?

It's hot all the year...
It's dark most of the day in winter...
There's a typhoon season...
There's a rainy season...

 E The weather is changing because of global warming.
What effect will this have?

ACTIVATING VOCABULARY – WEATHER

A   Compliments

I like your new tie.
That's a very smart jacket.
That suits you.
What a pretty dress.

Buying clothes

What size do you take?
Can I try this on?
Can I change this please?
It's a bit }
They're } long/tight/small/big.

Have you got this in green?
I'll have this one.
I'll leave it, thanks.

B   WORD CHECK

Look in the wardrobe below!

Find the 19 different clothes in the wardrobe.
(The five people in the picture are wearing these clothes)

Can you ALSO identify

shorts... cardigan... glasses... handkerchief...
tights... slippers... blouse... trainers? ...

C	O	A	T	J	A	C	K	E	T
S	H	I	R	T	P	A	N	T	S
D	G	L	O	V	E	P	X	V	I
R	Z	P	U	L	L	O	V	E	R
E	Z	J	S	O	C	K	S	S	I
S	H	O	E	S	B	E	L	T	N
S	C	A	R	F	H	A	T	I	G
B	R	A	S	K	I	R	T	E	E

C

What are you wearing at the moment?
What do you usually wear for
• a party?
• a picnic?
• to play sport?
• at work/school?

COLOURS
bright yellow
light blue
dark blue

MATERIALS
cotton
man made fibre
wool
silk

collar

sleeves

pocket
button

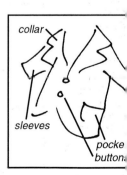

striped   *check*   *plain*   *patterned*

© **English Experience, 25 Julian Road, Folkestone, Kent, CT19 5HW**

WORD CHECK

I'm laying the table. Can you find a –
cup... teaspoon... glass... jug... plate...
bowl... fork... saucer... cloth... knife ...

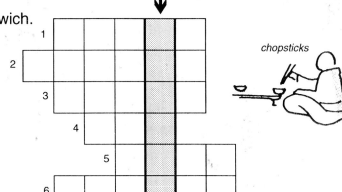

Do this **puzzle** and find an important piece of kitchen equipment.

1   You put food on it.
2   Salt and ...
3   Eat it on its own – or make a sandwich.
4   Water comes out of it.
5   It's not a knife.
6   You put it on 3.

chopsticks

Dinner with friends

Help yourself/Do start.
Would you like some sauce/salad?
Could you pass the salt/sugar please?
Mmm... This is lovely!
Would you like some more ...?
No thanks. It was absolutely delicious.

How things are cooked –
boiled, fried, baked, steamed, barbecued – and of course some things are eaten raw.
I am a vegetarian. Which of these things can I eat?
nuts – salad – steak – bacon – plums – lamb – biscuits – cheese – jam – fish

I like coffee.
I like tea.
I like sitting here
On your knee!

D   These are mixed up! Can you find the right definition?

cereal	sweet yellow sauce - often hot
strawberry	very expensive and delicious fish
prawn	sweet red fruit growing near ground
salmon	general word for things like cornflakes
curry	small shellfish - pink when you eat it
custard	hot, spicy way of cooking

E

Put the words into the right categories (5 in each)

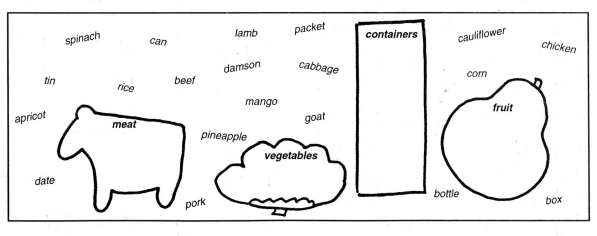

spinach   can   lamb   packet   **containers**   cauliflower   chicken

tin   rice   beef   damson   cabbage   corn   chicken

apricot   **meat**   mango   goat   **fruit**

pineapple

date   **vegetables**   bottle   box

pork

F   There are many different things to eat on this page. Which 4 would you like for dinner?

A WORD CHECK
Parts of the body.
Do you know these?
leg... shoulders... arm... knee...
hand... foot... chest... head...
elbow... toes... finger...

MR UNIVERSE
1ST PRIZE

B What are these?

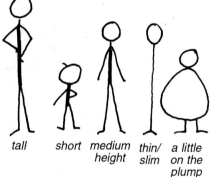

eyes... beard... neck... eyebrows...
curly hair... mouth... nose...
moustache... straight hair... ear...

C Describing people

tall   short   medium height   thin/ slim   a little on the plump side

AGE

baby   child
teenager   young person
adult   in her twenties
in his late forties   I'm getting on a bit

Style

casual   elegant   smart
scruffy   trendy

Relationships

single...married...separated...
divorced...living with...going out with...
engaged...widowed

LIKES   cars   dancing
sport   music   travel

Personality

hot tempered...
calm...shy...
absent-minded...
extrovert

D Emotions
How do you feel?   angry... in love... frightened... in pain... happy... sad... worried...

A WORD CHECK

dog... giraffe... bird... monkey... horse... rhino... penguin... cat... lion... snake... swan... seal... elephant... fish... ladybird... snail...

Which of these are **wild** animals (giraffe, lion) and which are **domestic** animals (horse, dog)?

B

Complete the word puzzle to find Safari Sam's favourite animal.

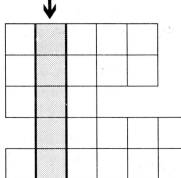

1 biggest thing in the sea
2 fierce, striped animal
3 large monkey
4 black and white - likes bamboo
5 rhymes with 'house'

Here's another animal ...

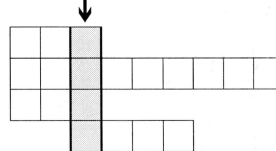

1 gives milk
2 not a friend of Captain Hook
3 night bird (very wise)
4 can swim and jump

C WORD CHECK

Do you know these?

wing... hoof (hooves)... teeth ... horns... beak... whiskers... tail ... mane... feathers... claws...

D I'm thinking of an animal. Ask questions to help you guess it.

Is it bigger than a cat/sheep/horse?
Is it brown/white/striped?
Does it have horns/a tail?
Does it live in England/hot countries/Africa?
Does it eat other animals?
Can it swim/climb trees/see in the dark?

Think of an animal and play the game with a friend.

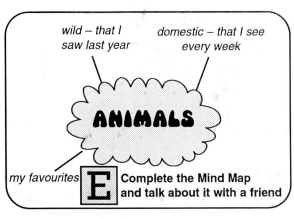

wild – that I saw last year   domestic – that I see every week

ANIMALS

my favourites

E Complete the Mind Map and talk about it with a friend

ACTIVATING VOCABULARY – ANIMALS

HOLIDAYS

A *Ask the person next to you:*

Did you go on holiday last year?
Where did you go?

"Wish you were here..."

I had
- a nice quiet relaxing holiday...
- a skiing/winter sports holiday...
- a camping/walking holiday...
- a sightseeing/touring holiday...

- by the sea.
- in the mountains.
- in the countryside.
- in northern Italy.

What did you do?
How did you spend your holiday?

We
- stayed at home.
- went to visit relatives.
- took the children to the sea.
- went by plane/car to...
- rented a cottage.
- hired a boat on the canals.
- went on a package tour.

Where did you stay?
How long did you stay?

We
- stayed in a hotel.
- stayed for a week.

What did you take?

I took
- warm clothes.
- swimming trunks/a bikini/
- a bathing costume.
- suntan oil.
- sunglasses.
- lots of luggage.

What was it like?

- It rained all the time.
- The weather was lovely.
- We had a really nice time.
- It was very interesting/enjoyable.
- I'll never go there again!

B **Have you ever had a holiday like this?**
It was cheap/expensive to stay there...lots to do in the evenings...a friendly atmosphere...
the people were very friendly...I took a lot of photos...went sightseeing...looked around the
museums...stayed for two weeks in a hotel...went swimming every day...drank a lot...taste
the local food...didn't like the food...couldn't speak the language...got a suntan...got sun-
burnt!...met a beautiful Swedish girl/fell in love with the waiter.

C **WORD CHECK**
What sort of holiday are these people having?

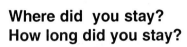

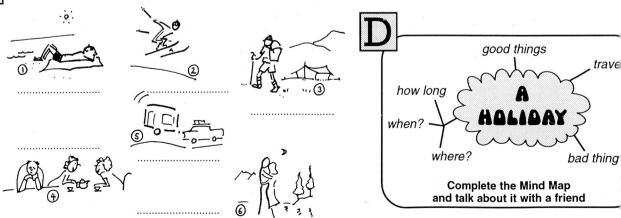

D

good things

trave

how long

when?

A HOLIDAY

where?

bad thing

**Complete the Mind Map
and talk about it with a friend**

A · WORD CHECK
What's it made of?

glass... wood... brick... stone... rubber... cardboard... cotton ... clay (pottery/china)... nylon...
What do you know that is made of metal? Of plastic?

B · What shape is it? Is it....?

oval - round - square - rectangular -
cylindrical - triangular - irregular

C · Some opposites – they are mixed up!
Can you make the right connections?

heavy	rare
expensive	shallow
sharp	flexible
tight	slow
colourful	cheap
genuine	weak
wide	light
deep	dull
common	blunt
strong	loose
rigid	hollow
fast	imitation
solid	narrow

D · I'm thinking of an object. Can you guess it?

Can you wear/carry/drink/move it?
Is it made of metal/paper?
Is it round/square?
Is it sharp/heavy?
Has it got a lid/a handle?

lid
handle

Play the 20 questions game with a friend.

E · Eight men and an elephant. Where are they?

in front of... inside... near... on.... behind... above...
a long way from... under...

How long/wide/high is it?

How deep/big heavy is it?
What's the diameter?

It's
{ 25cm long
5cm wide
20m high

It's
{ 2m deep
12² (square)m in area
6kg in weight
3cm in diameter

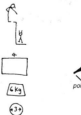

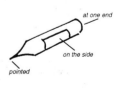

at one end
on the side
pointed

F · Can you describe these?

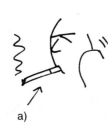

a)

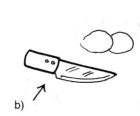

b)

c)

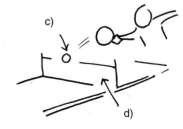

d)

A

What do you do? I'm a teacher/mechanic/shop assistant.

Where do you work?
- I work in a factory/an office.
- I work for ABC company.
- In my job I travel a lot/help sick people/ make decisions about.../sell.../mend...

Do you like your job?
- It's very interesting/boring/difficult/well paid/ poorly paid/enjoyable/hard work
- I deal with overseas clients/angry customers/ tourists/the technical side/people who want...

I'm a consultant in the tourism industry

B ODD ONE OUT

- cook – waiter – farmer – hairdresser
- pilot – mechanic – builder – electrician
- policeman – banker – traffic warden – referee
- book-keeper – accountant – engineer – cashier
- sales assistant – actress – model – clown
- lawyer – dentist – nurse – doctor
- receptionist – greengrocer – computer manager – watchman

"THE TOP"

director
manager
employee
trainee
getting promotion

C

These are mixed up! Can you make the right connections?

carpenter	takes orders in a restaurant
clown	controls the company finance
secretary	writes articles for magazines
detective	does operations in hospital
journalist	delivers letters
postman	uses a word processor
surgeon	makes people laugh
accountant	catches criminals
furniture remover	makes things from wood
waiter	helps people move to a new house

E

Complete the Mind Map and talk about it with a friend

D WORD CHECK

Where do these people work?
teacher ... caretaker ...
store manager ... mechanic ...
financial adviser ... mayor ...
surgeon ... sales assistant ...
cashier ... taxi driver ... cleaner ...
civil servant ... ticket clerk ...
receptionist ... flower seller ...
IT specialist ...

F

Interview your neighbour about the sort of job he/she has – or would like to have.

A We keep in touch in many ways, by talking, by writing, by e-mail.
All of **these** things are useful in communication. What are they?

sending (or getting) a fax ... writing (or getting) a letter ... sending (or getting) an email ...
making (or getting) a phone call ... leaving a message ...
calendar ... writing paper ... map ... stamp ... telephone directory ... diary ... envelope ...
ballpoint/pen/biro ... printer ... answerphone ... mobile (phone) ...

B

> *Complete this postcard (or email) to a friend –*
> *choose one word/expression from each box below*
> *(unfortunately the boxes are not in the right order!)*

AFFIX
STAMP
HERE

Dear....

I'm having.......... time here in.......... I'm staying at a............

in............ The weather is............. so/but I'm.............. a lot.

Yours,

a good
a terrific
an exciting
an interesting

Kenya
Alaska
Thailand
California

luxury hotel
camp site
caravan Site
safari park

the mountains
the north
near the sea
a very beautiful area

good
hot
snowy
wet

You can expand this by using some of these phrases:

Thanks very much for your card.
It's good to hear from you again.
I was very glad to hear from you again.
I'm very glad that you.....
I'm sorry to hear about....

You must come and visit us.
We may see you in.....
....sends his best wishes.
Best wishes to....

C Reply to this message you have just received from a friend:

Dear
Sorry I haven't written for a long time. I've been busy because I've got a new sales job which is hard work but very interesting. We've also just got back from holiday in Scotland; it was very enjoyable – until I broke my leg! Sarah sends her best wishes. I hope your parents are fit and well. I'm doing a lot of travelling in the new job so I may see you later in the year.
Yours,

A You don't look very well. What's the matter?

I feel { sick. / awful. / feverish. / dizzy. }

I've got a { high temperature. / cold. / sore throat. / headache. / pain in my.... / an infection. }

I've { cut my finger. / broken my leg. / hurt my shoulder. / twisted my knee. / bruised my arm. }

I'm sorry to hear that.

You'd better { see a doctor/have a check-up. / have a stiff drink. / go to bed. / take an aspirin/sleeping pill/pain killer. / put a bandage on it. }

How's your cold/headache? It's { still there I'm afraid. / getting better thanks. / much better now thanks. }

B WORD CHECK
What's number 3?   What's wrong with Mr 16?

CASUALTY

a cut ... stomach ache ...
nurse ... spots ...
sore throat ... needle ...
ambulance ... stretcher ...
Elastoplast ... medicine ...
crutches ...blood ... pills ...
sling ...black eye ...
bandage...

In Hospital: emergency, casualty department, operating theatre, have an operation, children's ward

C Put the words into the right categories (4 in each)

D What's wrong with *you*?

The doctor told you to:

- gargle with this three times a day...
- come back in three weeks to have the plaster off...
- stay out of contact with people for ten days...
- keep an Elastoplast™ on it and keep it dry for 48 hours...
- get back to work at once...

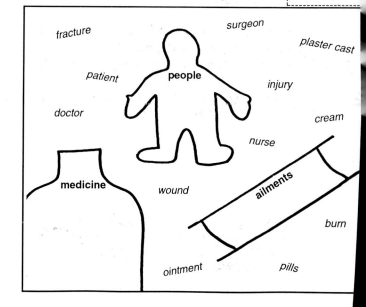

fracture · surgeon · plaster cast · patient · **people** · injury · doctor · cream · nurse · **medicine** · wound · **ailments** · burn · ointment · pills

ACTIVATING VOCABULARY – HEALTH

ANSWERS

B. Father-in-law/grandson/Tanya/wife/brother-in-law/aunt/cousins/niece/daughter-in-law/Yes. Miles
C. aunt/son/uncle/goldfish

A. 2 6 4 1 3 5

A. terrace 5 hut 3 castle 4 detached 2 palace 1 apartment 6
B. 1 window 2 front door 3 roof 4 chimney 5 satellite dish 6 garage 7 drive 8 path 9 wall 10 gate
C. 1 upstairs 2 downstairs 3 bedroom 4 kitchen 5 cellar 6 attic 7 dining room 8 toilet 9 bathroom 10 living room
   11 third floor 12 stairs 13 lift/elevator

A. 1 armchair 2 lamp 3 fireplace 4 ornaments 5 bookshelf 6 sofa 7 carpet 8 coffee table 9 rug 10 fridge
   11 microwave 12 fridge 13 washing machine 14 sink 15 tea towel 16 cooker 17 oven 18 dressing gown
   19 mirror 20 chest of drawers 21 hangers 22 wardrobe 23 curtain 24 pillow 25 sheet 26 blanket/duvet
   27 bedside table 28 bath 29 shower 30 toilet 31 sink 32 tap 33 greenhouse 34 fence 35 vegetable garden
   36 lawn 37 hedge 38 shed 39 flowerbed
B. cooker/chair/mirror/shed/sheet

A. 1 ambulance 2 lorry 3 bike 4 people carrier 5 bus 6 fire engine 7 coach 8 car 9 van 10 motorbike
   1 office block 2 row of houses 3 warehouse 4 factory 5 row of shops 6 bus station 7 church 8 building site
   9 apartment block 10 modern estate
B. zebra crossing/pavement/T junction/roundabout/speed bump • phone box post box litter bin cashpoint bus
   stop • hospital/Town Hall/school/police station/library • pedestrians/shoppers/motorists/cleaner/builder
C. 1 buying fruit 2 riding a bike 3 taking the dog for a walk 4 posting a letter 5 waiting for a bus
   6 pushing a baby buggy 7 talking/chatting 8 getting on a bus 9 getting off a bus 10 sitting on a bench
   11 looking in a window 12 making a phone call 13 crossing the road 14 driving a car

6 A. 1 hill 2 mountain 3 forest 4 river 5 bridge 6 waterfall 7 farm 8 field 9 woods 10 lake 11 stream
   1 muck heap 2 farm workers 3 tractor 4 farmhouse 5 stable 6 pond 7 barn 8 pigsty
B. oak/fir/ash/chestnut/beech • cabbage/beans/carrots/maize/rice • peaches/cherries/grapes/bananas pears •
   goat/sheep/buffalo/donkey/cow
C. trees/forest, sheep/flock, birds/flock, mountains/range, cows/herd, tourists/crowd

7 A. 1 cliff 2 castle 3 rocks 4 fishing boat 5 deckchair 6 seagulls 7 sunbathers 8 windsurfer 9 cloud 10 ferry
   11 sailing boat 12 lighthouse 13 harbour 14 hotels 15 lifebelt 16 pushchair 17 stall 18 horizon 19 island
   20 palm trees 21 mermaid 22 fish 23 speed boat 24 water skier 25 beach hut 26 beach 27 waves
B. ferry/container ship/rowing boat/yacht/tanker/liner • shells/seaweed/sand/wave/pebbles/tide • flippers/mask
   snorkel/sun lotion/towel/sunglasses • tuna/shark/octopus/crab/lobster/sea urchin

A. paperbag • leather handmade large • leather handmade large
B. 1 in a supermarket 2 carrying a basket 3 pushing a trolley 4 in a market 5 at the checkout 6 with a credit card
C. grocer – soup/cheese/spaghetti/olives • butcher – sausages/meat pie/steak/minced beef • baker – buns
   cakes/sliced bread/jam tart • newsagent – magazine/cigarettes/local paper/birthday cards • hardware – paint
   nails/light bulb/ladder

A. 1 weights 2 club 3 bat 4 net 5 baton 6 wicket 7 stick 8 pads 9 diving board 10 track 11 ring 12 court 13 pitch
   14 bowling alley 15 helmet 16 pool 17 winning post
C. ice hockey/basket ball/gymnastics/long jump/spectator sponsor

10 B. 1 collecting (stamps) 2 going to the theatre 3 sewing/dressmaking 4 hiking 5 playing badminton/squash
   6 listening to music 7 painting 8 cooking 9 playing chess 10 gardening 11 skateboarding 12 bird watching

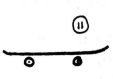

ACTIVATING VOCABULARY – ANSERWS 1

11 A. sunny rainy cloudy cold foggy windy snowy
B. Argentina (Buenos Aries) Canada (Montreal) - it's winter (January)
C. humid rainbow drought avalanche
D. Tropical countries/northern countries (Scandinavia)/Far Eastern countries/many African countries

12 B. 1 hat 2 scarf 3 glove 4 coat 5 shoe 6 skirt 7 cardigan 8 blouse 9 ring 10 dress 11 bra 12 tights 13 jacket
14 glasses 15 tie 16 pullover 17 trousers 18 slippers 19 handkerchief 20 cap 21 vest 22 belt 23 shorts
24 socks 25 shirt 26 trainers

13 A. 1 fork 2 plate 3 spoon 4 knife 5 cloth 6 bowl 7 saucer 8 cup 9 teaspoon 10 jug 11 glass
B. plate pepper bread tap fork butter – teapot
C. nuts salad plums biscuits cheese jam (fish?)
D. cereal – cornflakes • strawberry – redfruit • prawn – shell fish • salmon – expensive fish • curry – spicy
cooking • custard – sweet yellow sauce
E. Meat – goat/pork/chicken/beef/lamb • vegetables – cabbage/spinach/cauliflower/corn/rice • tin/box/can/pack
bottle • fruit – mango/damson/apricot/date/pineapple

14 A. 1 head 2 arm 3 shoulder 4 elbow 5 hand 6 finger 7 chest 8 leg 9 knee 10 ankle 11 toes 12 foot
B. 1 curly hair 2 eyes 3 nose 4 ear 5 mouth 6 beard 7 moustache 8 neck 9 eyebrow 10 straight hair
D. 1 sad 2 happy 3 angry 4 in pain 5 in love 6 worried 7 frightened

15 A. 1 bird 2 giraffe 3 rhino 4 lion 5 elephant 6 monkey 7 snake 8 penguin 9 seal 10 fish 11 cat 12 dog 13 swan
14 horse 15 snail 16 ladybird
B. whale tiger ape panda mouse – hippo • cow crocodile owl frog – wolf
C. 1 horn 2 tail 3 hoof 4 beak 5 wing 6 feather 7 mane 8 whiskers 9 teeth 10 claws

16 1 seaside – sunbathing 2 skiing – winter sports 3 camping – hiking 4 visiting relatives 5 touring – caravanning
6 romantic – sightseeing – honeymoon

17 A. 1 brick 2 rubber 3 cotton 4 clay (china/pottery) 5 stone 6 glass 7 cardboard 8 wood 9 nylon
B. 1 oval 2 cylindrical 3 triangular 4 irregular 5 rectangular 6 square 7 round
C. heavy – light expensive – cheap sharp – blunt tight – loose colourful – dull genuine – imitation wide – narrow
deep – shallow common – rare strong – weak rigid – flexible fast – slow solid – hollow
E. 1 in front of 2 on top of 3 above 4 under 5 inside 6 near 7 behind 8 a long way off
F. It's a cylinder made of paper. It's filled with tobacco. There's a filter at one end. It's about 5 cm long and 1 cm
in diameter. There's a (wooden) handle and a sharp metal blade. The ball is a hollow plastic sphere. The net
is rectangular and made of nylon.

18 B. hairdresser pilot engineer sales assistant lawyer greengrocer
C. clown/make people laugh secretary/word processor detective/criminals journalist/magazines
postman/letters surgeon/hospital accountant/finance furniture remover/new house waiter/restaurant

19 A. 1 sending an email 2 getting a fax 3 writing a letter 4 making a phone call 5 envelope 6 stamp 7 mobile
8 answerphone 9 telephone directory 10 map 11 pen 12 leaving a message 13 diary 14 printers 15 calendar

20 B. 1 bandage 2 black eye 3 sling 4 crutches 5 plaster 6 ambulance 7 stretcher 8 nurse 9 needle 10 patient
11 medicine 12 pills 13 a cut 14 blood 15 a plaster/Elastoplast 16 stomach ache 17 sore throat 18 spots
C. patient surgeon nurse doctor • pills ointment medicine cream • wound fracture burn injury

ACTIVATING VOCABULARY – ANSWERS 2